Finding Regina

finding REGINA

SHOSHANA SPERLING

Finding Regina
first published 2003 by
Scirocco Drama
An imprint of J. Gordon Shillingford Publishing Inc.
©2002 Shoshana Sperling

Scirocco Drama Series Editor: Glenda MacFarlane
Cover design by Doowah Design Inc.
Cover photo by Marina Dempster
Original art design by Field Day Inc.
Author photo by Graham Powell
Printed and bound in Canada

"Rae's Poem" on page 24 is by Suzanne Robertson and is reprinted with permission.

Published with the financial assistance of The Canada Council for the Arts
and the Manitoba Arts Council.

Production enquiries should be addressed to:
Playwrights Guild of Canada
54 Wolseley Street, 2nd Floor
Toronto, ON M5T 1A5
Phone 416-703-0201 e-mail pr@puc.ca

Canadian Cataloguing in Publication Data

Sperling, Shoshana
       Finding Regina/Shoshana Sperling
A play.
ISBN 0-920486-37-1

I. Title.
PS8587.P473F55 2003   C812'.6   C2003-900274-8
PR9199.4.S714F55 2003

J. Gordon Shillingford Publishing
P.O. Box 86, 905 Corydon Avenue, Winnipeg, MB Canada R3M 3S3

Dear Regina,

I miss you so much when I'm away from you. You don't feel that unless you leave but to all who have stayed: Shelly, Jason, Adam who returned, Dad, Maggie, Carrie, those newly finding like Alla, Sammy and Sofia...thanks for keeping it warm. And it is very warm. This play is for me and and also those still finding Regina way out in Toronto, Vancouver, Calgary, Montreal. This play goes out to Bruce Lund, Mike Tutt, Clint Hutchison, Seth Murry, Brent Cojacar and many more but mostly for Leo Lane. I wish you were here.

Sincerely,
Shoshana Sperling

Shoshana Sperling

Shoshana Sperling grew up in Regina and is now based in Toronto. For theatre, Shoshana has written and performed in many things, including: *The Golden Mile*, directed by Ed Sahely in the 1999 Toronto Fringe Festival and Buddies in Bad Times Theatre, *The Regina Monologues* for the Rhubarb Festival, *The Rise and Fall of Vella Dean*, and which was directed by Teresa Pavlinek at the 2001 Toronto Fringe Festival. She co-wrote and performed *Sheboobie* for Factory Theatre, Rhubarb Festival and the San Francisco Fringe Festival. Shoshana was a member of the Buddies in Bad Times and Theatre Passe Muraille writing units.

For radio and television Shoshana has written and performed in *The Golden Mile* on CBC Radio's *Sunday Showcase*, a CTV *Comedy Now* special, CBC Television's *Comics*, Vision TV's *Skylight* for three seasons, and co-wrote and performed in CTV's *The Jann Arden Special*. She hopes to finish a CD for children later this year.

Special Thanks

Ed Sahely for the love, original direction and dramturgy, Teresa Pavlinek for the steady and relentless eyes, encouragement and brilliance, wise Ed Roy, Kelly Thornton and Nightwood Theatre, Zöe Carpenter, Layne Coleman, Jacopa Knappen and the Passe Muraille writing unit, Lisa Brooke and all that we felt, Suzanne Robertson for Rae's poetry, Ann-Marie MacDonald, Jason Plumb, Meagan Lane, Sarah Kramer for endless support, Shelly Kambeitz, Troy Young, Jill Steadman, Dmitry Chepovetsky, Todd Falkowsky, Ralph Chapman, Diane Flacks, Sandra Alland, Ruth Madoc-Jones, Mariko Tamaki, Caroline Gillis, Jeremy Harris, Ali Eisner, steady Sonja and Deb Mills, Glenda MacFarlane, Gord Shillingford, Jann Arden, *NOW* magazine, my mom and dad for love and $upport, and the warm staff at the Globe Theatre and the Theatre Passe Muraille. Musical thanks to The Supers, Ben Folds, Jason Plumb, Andy Partridge and Martin Sexton for inspiration. My Army: Maury LaFoy for honesty, patience and love, Graham Powell, Teresa Pavlinek, Kathleen Schratz and Kate Huband for always being there and sharing all the depression. And my muse, Regina.

Production History

Finding Regina was first produced as *Finding My Regina* by the Globe Theatre in association with Nightwood Theatre and Theatre Passe Muraille and received its premiere on October 8, 2002, at the Globe Theatre, Regina, with the following cast:

> ANNABEL .... Shoshana Sperling
> RAE .... Teresa Pavlinek
> JOSH .... Jeremy Harris

> Directed by Kelly Thornton
> Dramaturged by Ed Roy
> Stage Manager: Zöe Carpenter

An earlier version of the play (*The Regina Monologues*) was workshopped in the Rhubarb Festival, February 21-25, 2001, at Buddies in Bad Times Theatre, Toronto, and featured the same cast but was directed and dramaturged by Ed Sahely and stage managed by Andrew Dollar. *Finding Regina* was workshopped May 6-9, 2002, with the same cast with Caroline Gillis as Annabel.

Scene One

Canadian? (handwritten)

Projection (handwritten, vertical left margin)

Music: "Cold as Ice" by Foreigner.

A slide of Canadian Prairies as seen out of an airplane window. Music is cut into by flight attendant's announcement.

ANNOUNCEMENT: Ladies and Gentlemen, we are about to make our descent into Regina. Please put your chair and table into the upright position to prepare for landing. The local time is 1:15 and the weather is sunny and clear. The temperature in Regina is presently –42. Please enjoy your stay and thank you for choosing Air Canada. We hope to see you again.

Slide of point-of-view inside of plane.

Mesdames et messieurs, nous sommes sur le point de transformer notre décent en Regina. Veuillez mettre votre chaise et table dans la position droite pour se préparer à l'atterrissage. Le temps local est 1:15 et le temps est ensoleillé et clair. La température dans Regina est actuellement –42. Nous vous espérons apprécions votre sejour dans Regina et vous remercions de choisir Air Canada. Nous espérons vous revoir bientot.

Screen goes white and white lights come up on waiting room.

JOSH, in parka, enters tthe waiting room. He sees no one and starts to leave. Changes his mind and sits down. Takes a bag of pot out and starts to roll a joint.

V/O of
ANNOUNCEMENT: Dr. Cornell to the ICU.

> *JOSH puts his pot away and sits. He then starts to exit again. ANNABEL comes in. She wears a parka. JOSH doesn't recognize her. They try to get by each other.*

JOSH: Excuse me.

ANNABEL: Josh?

JOSH: Yeah. (*JOSH is confused by her parka.*)

ANNABEL: Oh…

> *ANNABEL unzips and JOSH recognizes her.*

JOSH: Hey, when did you get in, Belly?

ANNABEL: About 20 minutes ago. I got my luggage as soon as I walked off the plane.

JOSH: You can't do that in Toronto.

ANNABEL: Yeah. My dad drove me straight here.

JOSH: Good on ya.

> *ANNABEL takes off her parka and starts to hang it up.*

ANNABEL: So, have you been in to see him yet?

JOSH: Not allowed. They only let in immediate family for right now. Intensive Care.

> *She goes to put coat on rack. Pause.*

ANNABEL: It's a cold one today.

JOSH: –78 with the wind chill.

ANNABEL: It never gets this cold in Toronto.

JOSH: No.

ANNABEL: We never get the wind like here.

JOSH: Yeah, the Peg is worse.

ANNABEL: The Peg.

JOSH: The Winterpeg.

ANNABEL: I haven't been away that long.

             Silence.

JOSH: Hey, so your dad got you from the airport?

ANNABEL: Yeah.

JOSH: That's cool.

ANNABEL: Wonder how long it'll be before I want to kill him.

JOSH: Yeah. You were always having some kind of fight with your old man eh? So, what's shakin' with your brother?

ANNABEL: Oh he's good.

JOSH: Yeah. Is he still partying hard? *(Chuckles.)*

ANNABEL: He's clean now. Thank God.

JOSH: Where's he been at these days?

ANNABEL: He's living in New York. Works at some design firm in Manhattan.

JOSH: Manhattan. Good on 'im.

ANNABEL: He does one of those jobs that you can't describe. One of those year 2003 ethernet/virtual jobs where *they* aren't sure what they do. He says, "Annabel, not advertising, I'm in ideas. Ideas, ideas—Ideas!" Capitalist. *(Beat.)* I got my dad's e-mail yesterday about Clarky. I forwarded it to everyone I could think of.

JOSH: That's cool.

> *Beat. ANNABEL looks towards Clarky's room.*

ANNABEL: I hope we get to see him.

JOSH: We will.

ANNABEL: My dad told me Clarky's liver was destroyed.

> *Pause.*

> Marnie Peshkin was sitting next to me on the plane and she told me...that he's a vegetable.

> *Pause.*

> Then the baggage claim guy, Ross, said they were going to amputate his hands and maybe his feet and that he might be a quadriplegic.

> *JOSH sits staring at the floor.*

JOSH: I don't think it's that bad. And it's Russ.

ANNABEL: That kid who was my frosh. I thought it was Ross.

JOSH: No. Ross is his twin but he does Parks and Rec so he's off for the next nine months. *canadian*

ANNABEL: Well...anyway that's what Russ told me.

JOSH: We're still waiting to hear.

> *Beat.*

ANNABEL: Is there a new billboard on Elphinstone? Near the old AB and D Mart?

JOSH: You mean the black sign with the fluorescent letters that no one reads?

ANNABEL: Yeah. God it's ugly.

JOSH: They're into it big time in the east end. (*Chuckling.*) And they still got that fake gorilla waving outside the Hill Billy Vac Shack.

ANNABEL: Oh yeah.

JOSH: You should blow by there and take a look.

ANNABEL: Can't wait.

JOSH: Hey, we could go for a drink later if you want?

ANNABEL: Yeah, that would be nice.

              RAE enters wearing a parka. Neither recognize her.
              She unzips.

JOSH: *(Seeing who it is and hugging her.)* Rae! Right arm!

RAE: God, it feels like –30 out there.

JOSH: –78 with the wind chill.

ANNABEL: Wind chill doesn't count. People out here just use it
              to sound heroic.

RAE: Oh my God Annabel! Wow. You look great.

ANNABEL: Compared to what? Ten years ago? Or I look great
              considering it's been ten years.

RAE: *(Laughs.)* That's so you Annabel. How's Clarky?

ANNABEL: Not good.

JOSH: We're still waiting to hear.

RAE: Are his parents with him now?

JOSH: They've been contacted. They live in Prince Albert
              now so they haven't got into town yet. Roads are
              bad I guess.

ANNABEL: Are you sure they're coming?

JOSH: They're his parents. Of course they're coming.

              Beat.

RAE: How… How did…

JOSH: He was running the Honda in the garage. Bottle of
                 Scotch, bottle of codeine mixed with
                 acetaminophen.

                 Pause. ANNABEL sighs.

RAE: My mother's thrilled to have the girls.

JOSH: Oh yeah, I heard you had kids.

RAE: Kiera's 6 and Rebbah, with a H. Rebbah's just 52
                 months.

JOSH: 12 months in a year…52 weeks…February has 28
                 days…carry the one (/)

ANNABEL: (/) Four and a half *(To RAE.)* in grown up years.

RAE: They're always babies to me. It's their first time in
                 Regina.

JOSH: No way.

RAE: Normally Robert thinks it's too cold for kids but
                 this time…well, he thought it would be good for
                 me and the girls to get away. He was going to be
                 working a lot anyway so… I never thought we'd
                 have to be here for Clarky. Can we go in and see
                 him?

ANNABEL
and JOSH: No.

JOSH: Intensive care. We're still waiting to hear.

RAE: I came straight from the airport… I couldn't make
                 the last one. Denise Alliston. Ringette team?

JOSH: Yeah. Played offence. It's cool that you could come.

RAE: Oh, I'm a Permi Parent at Kiera's school this year.

                 The other two stare at her.

                 In the private schools they ask that the parents put

in a certain amount of help time. You know…crafts and reading, swimming. But most parents only become Semi-Permi Parents. I guess they thought I'd be good as a Permi Parent.

ANNABEL: Like Premature?

RAE: No. As in Permanent Parent. All day.

ANNABEL: Mothers everywhere would be insulted to hear that someone has denoted a title to what women have been doing since they climbed out of their primordial dung.

JOSH: What?

RAE: So? How've you been Josh?

JOSH: Well…I got a good job at the record store downtown. The only one not owned by HIV. (*Chuckles.*) HMV… Blew my alternator about the first snow in October but the Pats are on a two-game winning streak. I'm doing fine. You?

RAE: I'm good.

JOSH: You look good.

RAE: Oh…thank you Josh. Well, I'm really happy.

JOSH: What's your guy do?

RAE: He works for a big architecture firm. Mostly in Beijing with a company called Quin to to…no Quin tan tan choo. Mother says that Robert is the ultimate provider. Me and the girls sing this song. (*Sings with hand gestures.*) Where's Daddy, Where's Dad. We take his good, his bad. He's the Dad. We love you this much. (*RAE stops a little embarrassed.*) Do I sound crazy?

ANNABEL: Yes.

JOSH: You still look great.

RAE: Oh Josh.

                ANNABEL looks offstage to CLARKY's room.

ANNABEL: I think his doctor's in there with him now.

RAE: Is he going to die?

JOSH: No.

ANNABEL: We don't know for sure.

RAE: Oh…I cancelled Rebbah's violin lesson…and I had
                to rearrange with Jonah's mom…another mom
                from school…not that I wouldn't have come…
                Oh…I would have waited… Oh Geez…

ANNABEL: Oh pooh! What if you don't get to wear your little
                black dress?!

RAE: Annabel!

JOSH: Must be a good five years now?

RAE: What?

JOSH: Since before Denise's funeral at least.

RAE: I'm sure it's not that long.

JOSH: We were all here for Teddy's wake about four or
                five years ago.

ANNABEL: I saw you last Christmas at The Free House.

JOSH: Don't remember that.

ANNABEL: You wouldn't. You were in celebration mode.

JOSH: *(Laughing.)* Yeah…

                Beat.

RAE: Robert and I are celebrating our new deck.

JOSH: Cool.

RAE: And we put in a Japanese Maple.

ANNABEL: I need to get some air.

RAE: You mean outside?

JOSH: Let's all go.

RAE: Isn't it –45?

JOSH: -78 with the…

ANNABEL: Stop calculating the wind chill.

JOSH: I can't. That's how we know what the temperature is. Wind chill is part of it.

ANNABEL: Wind chill is male.

RAE: Annabel, you're not in Toronto anymore.

ANNABEL: Neither of you have to come outside with me.

                She leaves. JOSH and RAE follow.

RAE: Is there a lobby? Or maybe a vestibule?

                Slides of Prairies, Regina settings. David Bowie's "Suffragette City" plays.

Scene Two

In the car. JOSH is rolling a joint.

RAE: I can't believe you still have this car.

JOSH: Two-door Chevy Monte Carlo, '76. Runs like a dream.

ANNABEL: If you plug her in.

JOSH is lighting up the joint.

JOSH: Hey Belly, wanna blow a tune on my little white trumpet?

Pretends to play the joint, passes it to ANNABEL.

ANNABEL: Here we go.

RAE: Where's your little brother these days?

ANNABEL: Please tell me he's not still calling bingo.

JOSH: He likes that they pay for his pants to get dry cleaned. He has this thing about dry cleaning. Makes him a hot shot or something.

They laugh. ANNABEL included.

RAE: *(Taking the joint and smoking.)* I'll pass. *(Still sucking on the joint.)* I haven't done drugs since high school. Other than cocaine. I haven't touched cocaine since the 90s. *(She giggles.)* How's your dad Annabel?

ANNABEL: You know, leftist rhetoric but the same sexist behaviour.

JOSH: I see your Dad in the summer riding his bike to

work. *(Laughing.)* He's got the big wool socks and then the sandals with his shorts. Hilarious.

ANNABEL: That style is very big on the runways of Albania.

JOSH and RAE laugh.

RAE: It's great to hang out again.

JOSH: *(To RAE.)* Yeah. It's really good to see you… Really you look fucking great. You haven't changed since Grade 12.

RAE: *(Giggling.)* Thanks Josh. *(Fiddles with her hair.)* I always look better in soft lighting. Those hospital lights are so aging.

JOSH: Is that why the ladies always want to stay in my car. And I thought it was the shocks. *(Laughs.)*

ANNABEL: To be honest this couldn't have happened at a worse time.

JOSH: Hey, we should blast by Houscum Pizza for old times sake and get a pie.

ANNABEL: I've got this dissertation…   *CNDIN*

RAE: Or what about Burger Baron for the Mushroom King Burger. Oh my God. Remember going for a burger at four in the morning?

ANNABEL: My thesis advisor is going to be so pissed off if I don't get my paper done.

JOSH: What? You're still in school?

ANNABEL: Yeah.

RAE: God. *(Laughing.)* I haven't read a book since… The 90s at least.

They laugh.

RAE: Are you still trying to get your degree?

ANNABEL: I'm finishing my masters in Womens' Studies.

JOSH: *(Laughing.)* I've been doing women's studies since I was two.

            They laugh.

ANNABEL: Actually, MA in Womens' Studies with a specialization in concepts of male and female archetypes in Western Civilization.

JOSH: I think I've seen that one at Blockbuster.

            Laugh.

ANNABEL: I've been working on my thesis for the past year.

RAE: That sounds fun.

ANNABEL: I don't know if "fun" is the word.

RAE: What's your thesis?

ANNABEL: Well, I believe that the classics which were written by women were misinterpreted by the patriarchal society. And that's what perpetuates our hierarchical gender structure.

JOSH: Is she speaking Greek? *(Laughs.)*

ANNABEL: Forget it.

            JOSH and RAE laugh.

RAE: No please Annabel...we wanna know. Do you mean like that women have written bad books about women?

ANNABEL: Noooo. Take Mary Shelley's *Frankenstein* for example.

JOSH: That was written by a chick?

ANNABEL: Yes. It's about man wishing to be God, or something that creates life like...? *(Looks at them.)*

C'mon... Woman. *(Beat of eye-rolling.)* The doctor wanted to be a giver of life but created a mutation of society itself, OK? So—Frankenstein—the monster—

JOSH: The monster and the doctor have the same name!

ANNABEL: Right, and the Frankenstein monster destroys everything it touches because of its deep agony of being alone.

RAE: I'm just hearing a dial tone.

JOSH: In the movie the monster roams around wrecking everything cause he wants to find another monster. A sexy monster.

                RAE laughs.

ANNABEL: See? Mainstream society appropriated that archetype, created by a woman that was critical of the patriarchy (/)

JOSH: (/) There she goes.

ANNABEL: (/) many archetypes have been exploited because of their inherent transmogratory nature for the patriarchy's own white bread ends. (/)...

JOSH: (/) OK so it has something to do (/) with food.

RAE: *(Laughing.)* (/) Josh...

JOSH: I almost forgot about the Annabel lecture circuit for the incredibly high.

                They laugh.

ANNABEL: Guys, it's simple. The castrated archetype that is harnessed for the feminist end, so lucidly delineated by Mary Shelley, is just turned into Kraft sandwich spread in the hands of patriarchy.

JOSH: She's actually starting to make sense to me. I better spark up another one. *(Lights another joint.)*

ANNABEL: So Rae, do you still write poetry? Or have you filled your head with tiny, whiny, nursery rhymes?

RAE: *(She recites:)*
"We are not now that strength which in old days
Moved earth and heaven, that which we are,
we are,—
One equal temper of heroic hearts,
Made weak by time and fate, but strong in will
To strive, to seek, to find, and not to yield."
Tennyson

ANNABEL: Not bad. Betcha can't do one of your own?

> RAE pauses and gets into the zone. She recites.

RAE: "All winter I waited for the boy
who never called.
The one who smelt of carbolic soap
and summer wind.
The only one I ever wanted to hold
plant a sunset in his mind,
and cure this longing,
this distance that stretches through
and beyond me,
where the lips of the earth
turn the sky red."

JOSH: Wow.

RAE: I've got the pot pasties. *(Laughs.)* I can't believe I remembered that.

ANNABEL: *(In awe.)* Me neither.

JOSH: That's hotter than talking with an Australian accent. I never knew you were into poetry?

ANNABEL: She was published in *Driftwood* and *The Prairie Dog* when she was sixteen.

JOSH: *(Putting his arm around her.)* I could write a book about what I was doing when I was sixteen.

ANNABEL: How titillating Josh. I'm sure you think an STD is a kind of motor oil. When it starts to itch, go to the gas station.

                  Girls giggle.

JOSH: Uh…no egghead. That's STP.

RAE: So you study stories about women.

ANNABEL: Kind of.

JOSH: *(Chuckles.)* Like I said, I've got some women's stories I could tell you.

ANNABEL: Oh like The Hammer, Josh? *(Beat.)* You remember her? At a party she had sex with six or seven boys. One entering her room, leaving a bit of himself and then making room for the next. I don't know if the others watched. The story goes that after all those men she was still not satisfied and so in the pain of being unfulfilled of her passion, she asked…no begged for a hammer to be put inside her. We were only to imagine which end would suffice.

RAE: I never believed that story.

ANNABEL: Josh?

JOSH: How would I know?

ANNABEL: Or what about The Flute. She was changing for gym class. Just coming from band practice, her flute was warm and still wet with her own spittle. (/)

RAE: (/) OK Annabel. (/)

ANNABE: (/) She was stumbled upon by a group, while masturbating with her instrument. *(Beat.)* Ah, Regina.

JOSH: It rhymes with what you think it shouldn't.

RAE: Why would anyone want to remember those stories?

ANNABEL: I might ask why one would want to forget.

RAE: Robert says there's only five real stories and the rest are copies.

JOSH: No way. Only five? Shit I can count at least that many on one hand… *(Laughs.)* get it…one hand… *(Looks at his hand.)*

RAE: That's why he hates going to movies and reading novels. I mean he reads… Robert is a reader…it's just that he likes biographies or you know…true stories of OJ or Bill Clinton.

ANNABEL: Uh…you mean…no movies…fiction…you've always loved that stuff. Don't you find that a bit…

JOSH: *(Cough.)* BORING!

RAE: No! My relationship is not boring. The other day I hit Robert in the head with an axe.

ANNABEL: What?

RAE: In C.C.

JOSH: Is that like the 4-H club or something?

RAE: C.C. Couple Counseling.

JOSH: They let you bring an axe into your therapy?

ANNABEL: That must sort out a lot of the little stuff right away.

RAE: No…no… It was my turn to bash him in the head with the axe.

ANNABEL: I knew Vancouver had a lot of alternative healing but (/)…

RAE: (/) It's not real. It's completely safe because it's totally made of Nerf.

JOSH and
ANNABEL: Nerf. *(Laughing.)*

RAE: Robert's great.

ANNABEL: So why are you going to counseling?

JOSH: Trouble in the bedroom?

RAE: No!

ANNABEL: So…

RAE: We're trying to change our Dance.

JOSH: What was wrong with the old one?

ANNABEL: Oh God no. You're not talking about the Dance of Anger are you?

RAE: Oh you've heard of it. It's great. That and the Artists Way, Part 3: This Time it's Personal. Everyone should read them. We all have our dances and sometimes we have to change them.

ANNABEL: So what's my dance? Oh oh I'm doing a salsa or no flamenco would be more my thing. I've got it! I'm busting a move. Yo yo!

RAE: You know why people have trouble falling in love, Annabel? Because they're looking for the right person but they don't know what they want. That's the dance of confusion.

ANNABEL: That's crap. It's all about looks. We're conditioned to believe that if we find a mate with ideal physical beauty, then we'll fall in love.

JOSH: So I don't have a girlfriend cause I like tits and I can't dance?

ANNABEL: No. My point is that we find this person "perfect"
                cause they're *(To JOSH.)* "hot," so we get married,
                kids, and then…

RAE: And then…

JOSH: Then… What happens?

ANNABEL: There's no intimacy. We stop being interested
                cause the whole thing was based on looks. Then we
                have to face the music or take dance lessons.

JOSH: But I can't not like tits. *(He drums.)* Tits tits tits. (/)

ANNABEL: I'm just saying that some people, not all, but…most
                people who grow up being splendidly beautiful
                might find themselves in a relationship that might
                be splendidly empty.

RAE: Are you saying…?

JOSH: Uh guys, we should go back in case there's news on
                Clarky.

                *"I Don't Know" by The Replacements plays. Slides
                of outdoors in Regina.*

Scene Three

Stoned in the waiting room. They all enter and JOSH offers a mickey to RAE.

RAE: *(She takes it and starts to drink.)* Really, here? In the hospital? Oh no. I haven't drank...

ANNABEL and JOSH: Since the 90s.

All laugh.

RAE: The last time I was here...

ANNABEL: It was for a funeral. Teddy Krulack.

RAE: That's right. How did you know that? You weren't even here.

ANNABEL shrugs.

Why do so many people from Regina try to kill themselves?

ANNABEL: I think your answer lies in your question.

JOSH: You dated Teddy for awhile right?

RAE: About two years. God he was cute. And smart. That guy had everything together.

JOSH: Seemed that way.

ANNOUNCEMENT: Doctor Badoo please report to obstetrics.

All look at each other and laugh.

RAE: Badoooo. *(Giggling.)*

She pulls up her sleeve and holds it out for JOSH.

RAE: Tickles...

ANNABEL: You still love tickles. What's with that?

JOSH takes her arm.

JOSH: I like tickles. Nothing wrong with tickles.

RAE: I used to make my little sister tickle me for a quarter. She was pretty good.

JOSH: That is hot.

ANNABEL: Her sister.

JOSH: I know. Hot.

RAE puts her feet in JOSH's lap.

RAE: Would you mind? It's almost a three hour flight from Vancouver and... *(Pauses then recites.)* The weight of a thousand nations has taken a rest break on my weary heart.

All laugh.

RAE: Well fuck me. I'm pissed. No. I'm wrecked. Toasted. Trashed. Totalled. *(Takes a swig. Coughs.)* My throat is ratched.

JOSH: You were just givin' 'er on that dubie. One haul was never enough for you.

JOSH and RAE laugh.

ANNABEL: Hey... Whatever happened to Leon Coen?

RAE: Leon Coen...

ANNABEL: Another member of the massive Jewish population in Regina.

JOSH: Leon did some fucked-up tour of Egypt, didn't bathe for weeks and his pubes grew through his underwear.

RAE: Fur gotch.

                All laugh.

ANNABEL: How do you know all that?

JOSH: I know everything about everyone in Red China. Reggie.

ALL: Vagina, Saskratchyerbum. *(All laugh.)*

JOSH: Everyone knows me and I know all of them. Most of them intimately. And just when it seems like I've been with all of them, their little sisters grow up. I think I help them find themselves.

ANNABEL: So you provide a service? Like Medicare?

JOSH: Hey, no one forces them to come to Josh's Farm. Every night after last call, I invite whose-ever's left at the Free House, to come over. We stay up all night playing guitar and just enjoying. It's not usual that I'd be sleeping alone. That's how I know the poop on everyone. It won't be the same if…

ANNABEL: Clarky and I used to write letters to each other after high school. I still have his Grad photo in my wallet. Says something like, "Think of me when you masturbate."

JOSH: That's Clarky. *(Laughing.)* Yeah.

ANNABEL: Once when we were on acid, we stood in front of the sandwich counter at the 7-Eleven all night trying to figure out the difference between a Hoagie and a Herbie. Laughing our asses off. We kind of lost touch.

                JOSH looks at ANNABEL. She gets up.

JOSH: Hey did you guys ever hear about Genie Davidson? She became a nun.

RAE: No!

JOSH: Wait. Then she leaves the church and becomes a puck.

RAE: Puck?

ANNABEL: *(Laughing.)* It means she has sex with hockey players.

JOSH: She must have really missed getting it. She did the whole team. Hey, did you hear about that hooker, Indian girl who was killed by some guys from Campbell?

RAE: I hated that school.

ANNABEL: So, what happened to the guys?

JOSH: Off on good behaviour.

ANNABEL: Oh Jesus.

JOSH: Claimed it was due to her being drunk and, you know…the Indian problem…

ANNABEL: Can you say Native or indigenous or First Nations?

JOSH: What for? We've always said Indian.

ANNABEL: I know but Indian refers to East Indian or from India (/) because the explorers thought they had found India when they found North America so…

JOSH: (/) Yeah yeah I know but we've always said Indian. You know I don't mean like Gandhi from India. I mean from…Fort Qu'appelle. From Kindersley, White Bear Lake or Saskabush. I mean from Regina. What, are you all politically correct now? How many Indian friends do you have in Toronto?

ANNABEL: That's different. It's Toronto. It's not like here. Right Rae? Vancouver must be the same.

RAE: Uh…we have… White people in Vancouver. Lots

of white people. And lots of Asians. Robert calls it Hongcouver.

ANNABEL: Hongcouver?

JOSH and RAE laugh.

JOSH: OK, but there must be Indians in Vancouver. I know guys who've moved there from here.

RAE: Maybe but not where I go.

JOSH: See. And what about in high school? Did you have any Indian friends?

RAE: No. It's not that I was against it. I just didn't.

ANNABEL: Tim Lablonde. He was Native.

JOSH: He was Métis. That doesn't count.

ANNABEL: I bet it counts to him. *(Remembering.)* Henry… First Nations. He was adopted by a white family.

RAE: Who?

ANNABEL: Remember we all went to that huge barn party near Lumsden and he gave out oil tokes?

JOSH: Moved back to the reserve. He wants to get back to his roots. Got all these protests going at the Legislative Building. About cops taking Indians for walks out on the highway and leaving them there. Couple guys died. Because of Henry, I don't think they're allowed to train their dogs to attack Indians anymore.

ANNABEL: Jesus. I saw something about that on the news.

JOSH: Slept with his cousin.

RAE: Jesus.

JOSH: I've had my fair share of Indian girls in high school. Yum City.

ANNABEL: I love the way you describe people. Is that how you talk about us when we're not around?

JOSH: *(Sings.)* Paranoia big destroya!

RAE: I think I saw Colin Sandason on my way over here. Walking across the foot bridge…

JOSH: Colin Sandason. Was in Honduras. Then moved to Las Vegas. Now he's back here. Sometimes he plays hockey at our rink. I know about everybody. Ask me about anyone? C'mon, ask me!

RAE: Where's Greg Good now?

JOSH: Moved to Barrie, Ontario to be a doctor.

ANNABEL: Gerry Burns.

JOSH: Got into some fucked-up thing with a girl on a reservation, her brothers dragged him from the back of their truck then cut him into pieces and boiled him.

ANNABEL: Sounds more like the *X-Files* than Regina.

RAE: Do you guys remember that… Gang or group or something. Oh God… I've got breast-feeding memory.

ANNABEL: But you're not breast-feeding.

JOSH: She's drunk and high but I like it when she calls it that. Breast-feeding.

RAE: Shit…what were they called? Native girls. They used to wait in the malls and when they saw a pretty blonde girl they would grab her and take her to the bathroom and what…

JOSH: Tomboy 16. They would slice her here *(Shows from the corners of his mouth on both sides.)* with an X-Acto knife, to make her have a permanent smile.

RAE: No. Tomboy 14 'cause they're were 14 of them.

JOSH: It was Tomboy 15 for sure 'cause they were all 15 years old.

ANNABEL: C'mon! It's totally a racist myth.

JOSH: Hey, believe what you want but that's the story.

ANNABEL: Just by telling it you're perpetuating the myth.

RAE: Uh… Spiro Coriandolis…

JOSH: Spiro Christitus and Grant Coriandolis…took over their dad's restaurants. One in the north end and one in the south. Shit. Other way around. Anyway—

ANNABEL: Cheryl from student council.

JOSH: Burt Egerhause gave her crabs so she married his best friend who was also named Burt.

RAE: Love that.

JOSH: I dated her sister. Man, I could go all night. Population 200,000. And dropping every 15 minutes. I still play hockey with some of the same guys from my midget team. Wait till they find out about Clarky.

RAE: It's going to be hard for them.

ANNABEL: Nah. They're from Regina. They'll just keep playing.

JOSH: Keep askin'!

ANNABEL: Evan…you know…had a twin…

JOSH: Evan Kalitis. Jumped off the TD Bank building before it merged with Canada Trust.

RAE: The wake was at the Teachers' Club.

JOSH: And you say pot rots your memory. Ask!

ANNABEL: Ok, what about...Patrick Dejarden? He went to Sheldon. Really cute.

RAE: Oh yeah. *(RAE puts her feet back into JOSH's lap. He rubs her legs in a more sexual way. ANNABEL looks on.)*

JOSH: Parents were schizo. Granddad was famous though no one ever knew why. Serious alcoholic.

RAE: Sounds bad coming from you. *(Giggle.)*

JOSH: Walked in front of a train.

RAE: Accident?

JOSH: Not when you leave a note. Rae, you were at that wake.

RAE: You must have dreamed me there. I missed that one. *(Flirt.)*

ANNABEL
and RAE: Soula Crouse! Homeroom 4 Zeus! *(Laugh.)*

JOSH: Drinking and driving accident near Prince Albert. Froze to death. They found her sitting straight up 100 feet from the car. She mighta lived if anyone had driven by. Slept with her. Not that night. *(Laughs but the girls do not.)*

RAE: So? *(Flirting with JOSH.)* I dated the train guy! *(Giggle.)*

ANNABEL: Yes but did you sleep with him?

RAE: No! I didn't sleep with anyone till Grade 12.

JOSH: Who got your cherry?

ANNABEL: Jealous?

JOSH: Yah right!

RAE: You guys remember when I was dating Trevor Leont?

JOSH: You gave it to Trevor? C'mon!

RAE: His older brother. *(Laughs. Flirting with JOSH.)* He was 30 and it didn't hurt a bit.

JOSH: So, you dated all those guys all through high school and you lose it to some old guy?

RAE: I'm 30 now.

ANNABEL: That's not old.

JOSH: It just seems like a waste that's all I'm sayin'. *(Remembering fondly.)* Shit, I had a hell of a lot of sex back then. Damn. I had our whole graduating class...well, with the exception of you two ladies, of course.

ANNABEL: Should I be insulted or flattered?

JOSH: C'mon, you guys were my friends.

RAE: Not that you didn't try with me. Mmmm... *(She leans into JOSH and runs her hand along his chest.)*

ANNABEL: Excuse me. I meant that I wasn't sure whether I should be insulted or flattered that you can't remember having sex with me.

RAE: You're kidding.

> *RAE slowly removes herself from JOSH and moves over to the coat rack.*

JOSH: Oh... Yeah. That's right... It was...uh...fun.

ANNABEL: Fun. Huh. You had whisky dick. You could barely keep it up. Thankfully I was on mescaline. The earth moved.

JOSH: I was still working on my technique. Belly, I'm

sorry; I had a lot of sex back then. *(Laughs.)* I don't remember.

ANNABEL: You don't remember? Aren't you a big man with all that sex it gets difficult to keep it all straight. I haven't smoked quite as much pot as you have. Let's see if my memory's any better for it. I remember when I made a pact with the boy down the street because I wanted to lose my virginity. Late one drunken night we tried in the back seat of his Malibu. Then we tried on his kitchen floor but his older brothers stumbled in. They patted him on the back and went to their beds. Finally, on the pull-out couch, only half pulled out, we had sex. We had sex for one year. But not looking as girls should look, it was kept a secret. Boys tell their adventures. Unless they're embarrassed. For my birthday, he took me for a long drive and I learned about fellatio. I felt warm liquid coming out my nose and thought I had a nose bleed. Sperm.

RAE: God Annabel. Do you have to talk like that?

ANNABEL: *(Meanly to RAE.)* His girlfriends were tall, thin and perfect. *(To JOSH.)* I never had a boyfriend. Let's see, I fucked Greg Good, Gerry Burns in his car right next to the smoking doors, Spiro Christitus and Grant Coriandolis, one of the Hatsitoliouses in TC Douglas Building Parking lot, Burt Egerhause pre-crabs, Patrick Dejarden in Tibits Park right outside of where his dad would jerk off at himself in the mirror.

RAE: That's disgusting.

ANNABEL: Girls wanted to have sex but they were so worried for their reputations. I never worried about any of that because... No one ever told. They just came back for more. I practiced this behaviour into my university years until I finally moved out of Regina. And the neighbour, my first time? My first love. Shot himself in the head five years ago last month. I heard about it by e-mail. Some things you don't forget.

RAE: You slept with Teddy…My Teddy? But he was (/)

ANNABEL: (/) Out of my league?

RAE: My boyfriend. He was cheating…with you?

ANNABEL: According to Teddy the farmers weren't the only ones having a drought.

RAE: I wouldn't have sex with him so he fucked my best friend.

ANNABEL: Yes, I guess that's how it started.

RAE: All that time you were lying to me. I can't believe it.

ANNABEL: Sometimes right from your place to his actually.

RAE: You and Teddy.

ANNABEL: What does it matter now?

RAE: It matters!

ANNABEL: You're shocked that he picked me over you.

RAE: Picked you…?

ANNABEL: Right. He just fucked me. Maybe he loved me. (*Beat.*) God, sometimes I'd hope you'd find out. That you'd walk right in on us and see us. Then everyone would know—

RAE: How could you do that to me? Right under my nose?

ANNABEL: It was a million years ago. What difference does it make now?

RAE: But Teddy… (/)

ANNABEL: (/) Is dead and you're married to Boring. I mean Robert.

RAE goes to JOSH and takes whiskey.

JOSH: Wow, you had more sex than I did.

ANNABEL: And I slept with Clarky.

JOSH: No way. He never told me.

ANNABEL: He didn't tell you a lot of things.

JOSH: But we play hockey together.

ANNABEL: Do you want to know why Clarky wants to kill himself? Because he's tired of getting blow jobs from old men in Wascana Park in –78 with the wind chill.

JOSH: What?

ANNABEL: Clarky's gay.

JOSH: That's bullshit! I know everything about that guy. We smoke up everyday. He helped me install my hot water pipes for fuck's sake. You don't know dick! You're just making shit up.

ANNABEL: He told me in high school.

JOSH: High school? Why would he tell you?

ANNABEL: And who else would he tell? You? Everyday you had a new fag joke. God, there's a fucking heterosexual Pride Day here. I'm surprised he lasted as long as he did in this stupid shit-ass town.

JOSH grabs his coat and heads for the door.

ANNABEL: *(Grabs her coat. Going after him.)* Josh…Josh!

Slides of Regina.

Scene Four

JOSH is sitting in his car flicking his lighter. ANNABEL sits next to him freezing.

ANNABEL: Josh, I can't take you being mad at me today.

JOSH: I'm not mad.

ANNABEL: Good because I'm the one who should be mad at you anyway.

JOSH: You? You're the one who's saying all that shit to me for no reason. I'm the one who's mad.

ANNABEL: You didn't remember having sex with me. Do you know what a gross feeling that is?

JOSH: Alright Belly.

ANNABEL: I mean at least you should remember when you do it with friends. I can understand forgetting the prostitutes.

JOSH: Hey, no hookers, OK?

ANNABEL: Only for special occasions right?

JOSH: OK already. I'm sorry. I forgot. You know if you'd put a pillow behind your head it would have jogged my memory. Joking.

ANNABEL: I know. *(Shivers.)* All this coming in and going out and skin freezing after being exposed for more than 30 seconds...

JOSH: Actually, skin'll freeze in 20 seconds or even 10. Just depends on the season.

ANNABEL: Well, I hope it's the winter season.

JOSH: You are cold. C'mere. *(She moves over to him and he starts warming her as he talks.)* Yeah. Well it mostly is the winter season here anyway. I mean just within that season of winter there's different seasons like say, super cold plug in the car or super massive cold with the cramp you get in your stomach from shivering or then like super massive ultra freezing cold when the water in your eyes...

ANNABEL: I get it. The seasons of winter.

JOSH: When your pee stream freezes outside it's called (/)

ANNABEL: What?

JOSH: Humongatory Frozanation.

    ANNABEL laughs.

    No really. And you know when even after you're warm in bed and your ass is still like a fucking iceberg floating around under the covers, well that my friend is called drinking weather...

    They begin kissing.

JOSH: Here lift up. *(Puts his hand under the bottom of her parka.)* You're still cold. This is how we warm up in these parts. *(More moving.)* And these parts. *(His hand is up her parka.)*

    Beat. They try to unzip each other's parkas. They struggle.

ANNABEL: The zipper's stuck.

JOSH: So's yours.

    They both try at their own. ANNABEL gets hers undone. She goes back to JOSH's which is stuck. Finally it opens and they embrace.

JOSH: That's better. You're not so cold here.

             He pulls her on top of him behind the wheel.

ANNABEL: You have snow on your boots.

JOSH: It'll melt.

ANNABEL: Here, lean this way.

             They shift so that he is on top. He puts both hands under her top and works his way to taking off her bra.

JOSH: How many hooks do you have on this thing?

ANNABEL: Four.

JOSH: It's like my hockey equipment.

ANNABEL: Let me get it.

             They stare at each other while she struggles with her bra. She undoes it.

ANNABEL: There.

             He puts his head under her shirt. Good times.

ANNABEL: *(Into it.)* Josh.

JOSH: Mmmmm...

ANNABEL: Josh...Josh. We need to stop doing this.

JOSH: I found a cold spot.

             He continues.

ANNABEL: Mmmmm... No, I really think... Ah... *(She closes her eyes and then opens them again.)* ...Josh.

JOSH: I'm workin' here.

ANNABEL: ...this is not what I want to be doing right now...Josh...

JOSH: Present.

ANNABEL: No seriously Josh… God I annoy myself…I'm not even back one day ….

              He is moving slowly under her shirt.

JOSH: We're just taking our minds off all this depressing shit…

ANNABEL: Stop OK?

JOSH: It's OK to feel good.

ANNABEL: You don't have to prove to me that you and Clarky weren't together.

              He stops cold.

JOSH: Sorry? (*JOSH pulls his head out of her shirt.*)

ANNABEL: It's OK to love another man without him being your lover.

              Gets off her abruptly.

JOSH: What the fuck? Jesus! I'm not a fag.

ANNABEL: Whoa. Easy.

JOSH: You're crazy.

ANNABEL: I can't believe that you didn't know he was gay. Didn't you ever wonder why he didn't have a girlfriend?

JOSH: I don't have a girlfriend.

ANNABEL: OK what about his family? Why aren't they here? He's in the hospital but the three of us are the only ones here. That doesn't strike you as strange?

JOSH: No.

ANNABEL: His family doesn't speak to him anymore. Didn't you ever wonder why that might be?

JOSH: He told me that they had a fight about the Buick.

ANNABEL: A car?! I think you knew Clarky was gay.

JOSH: That's fucked!

ANNABEL: No... What you're feeling is OK...

JOSH: I'm not feeling anything. I was just about to have sex with you and I couldn't do that if I was a cocksucker now could I!?

ANNABEL: God Josh, you might try sucking a little cock! It's not so bad.

JOSH: Fuck you, Annabel.

JOSH exits. ANNABEL pauses, then exits.

Music. Slides.

Scene Five

ANNABEL enters and walks toward the ICU. She stops. RAE has been drinking the whole time.

RAE: That was quick. I'm impressed.

ANNABEL: Shut up.

RAE: Where's Josh?

ANNABEL: Gone for a walk.

RAE: But it's –78 with the (/) wind chill.

ANNABEL: (/) Shut up about the fucking wind chill for Christ sake!

RAE: Don't talk to me like that.

            ANNABEL starts to leave again.

            Going somewhere?

ANNABEL: I'll come back later.

RAE: When no one's here to bother you? You're just the same. Run, run, Annabel, and maybe you won't have to take responsibility for anything or anyone.

            ANNABEL stops.

ANNABEL: I'm just trying to survive another trip to Regina.

RAE: Poor Annabel. You're the one that makes it so difficult. You didn't have to have sex with my boyfriend. Did you ever think that I may have loved him?

ANNABEL: But you didn't.

RAE: Don't tell me what I felt. You proved you could have any guy you wanted. Teddy, Josh, Clarky. You fucked them all, Annabel. Why Teddy? I'll tell you why. Because it wasn't about sex. It was about power...you used sex to get power over them. Just to prove you could. Just to prove you could get any guy that the pretty girls could get. One for the underdogs. You were just jealous because I had a choice and you didn't. I was smart enough to do what you were doing but I was pretty enough to not have to do anything at all. You thought I was shallow. Having men buy me drinks. Some men as old as my father. Guys took me out and bought me Oscar de la Renta perfume. It wasn't my fault. I was flattered. I was 17, for God's sake.

ANNABEL: Bullshit! Every guy in our school wanted to sleep with you. You were the one who couldn't last a day without a boyfriend.

RAE: Teddy was a conquest for you wasn't he, and maybe if my best friend didn't seduce him we would be together right now and he'd be here.

ANNABEL: What? Are you...saying that it's my fault that Teddy killed himself?! I wasn't even in town.

RAE: Oh that's right, maintaining friendships never fit into your schedule.

ANNABEL: I can't believe you would say that to me. When you're the one who dumped me for the lawyers and the football players and the cocaine.

            Pause.

RAE: Is that why you hate me so much? Was I so horrible to you? We were going to be old ladies still smoking pot and crying at bad movies. Talking about nothing and loving every minute. You didn't even come to my wedding. You could have stayed friends with me, Annabel.

ANNABEL: You were the beautiful one. I was the sidekick. I didn't fit into your perfect new life and I don't fit into it now.

RAE: Perfect life! Now that my uterus has fallen onto my bladder and I cross my legs half the day so I don't piss? Stretchmarks? Electrolysis on my nipples? My perfect husband can't stand to see me naked. He tells me to go to the gym and do something with my hair. My kids are both obsessive compulsives and today is the first time I've been away from them since they were born so it's not so perfect.

ANNABEL: What do you want from me?

JOSH enters.

JOSH: I'm not gay.

ANNABEL: The whole world knows that.

RAE: Robert left me.

JOSH: Your husband left you?

RAE: Someone from work. He shopped up for a better model. Like our BMW. She's very fit and clever.

ANNABEL: That's not my problem. You picked the wrong person to rescue you.

JOSH: Tell us about rescuing people, Annabel.

ANNABEL: What, you mean not helping your best friend even though you knew he was gay? While you were fucking somebody's sister, he was drunk in the corner or having anonymous sex in goose shit park.

JOSH: You're fucking rank!

ANNABEL: You never had to look at your own life and what
             you weren't doing as long as you had a buddy
             doing it with you. Making you feel like it was OK to
             be here. To still be acting like you were in high
             school. Right Josh?

JOSH: Leave it, Annabel.

ANNABEL: Never drink alone. And Clarky? He's the only real
             relationship you've ever had outside of your
             family. The most important relationship in your
             life is with a gay man. You love a gay man. He
             didn't try to kill himself because he was gay. It's
             cause he was alone. With you everyday and totally
             alone.

JOSH: He called you!

ANNABEL: And...and so what do you do? You fuck
             everything in town as fast as you can to prove that
             you aren't like him. A fag.

JOSH: He called you. I know.

ANNABEL: You know the gossip. (*ANNABEL grabs her coat and
             goes to exit.*)

JOSH: I know he called you two days ago.

RAE: What?

ANNABEL: No! That's bullshit coming from some
             homophobic... (/)

JOSH: Two days ago and you didn't call him back.

RAE: What's he talking about?

ANNABEL: He's making it up. (*Gathering her coat.*)

JOSH: It wasn't me that he called looking for help. You're
             the one that bailed on Clarky. And it was me that
             followed the ambulance.

RAE: What do you mean?

ANNABEL: I hadn't heard from him in so long. I didn't even
                recognize his voice...

JOSH: Bullshit!

ANNABEL: We just lost touch and then all of a sudden there
                was this voice on my answering machine. OK?!

RAE: And what did you do?

ANNABEL: I...I was... I was in the middle of a stressful week
                and...

JOSH: What did you do Annabel?

ANNABEL: It's not like it would have made a difference.

JOSH: What did you do when you heard the message
                from Clarky?!

ANNABEL: I erased it.

RAE: Oh God.

ANNABEL: Don't do that. How was I supposed to know?

JOSH: Brutal.

RAE: How did he sound?

ANNABEL: Drunk. Happy...

RAE: Happy?

ANNABEL: Yeah. The time of his life.

JOSH: Why didn't you call him back? He was there for
                you, Belly.

ANNABEL: I told you I hadn't heard from him in along time.

JOSH: Then it must have been important.

ANNABEL: We weren't friends anymore. It wasn't my
                responsibility...

JOSH: But you were friends the summer after high school? Before you moved to Toronto. Remember that summer?

RAE: What are you talking about?

ANNABEL: Shut up Josh. You don't know...

JOSH: You were here that summer and lucky for you so was Clarky.

RAE: I was here then too.

ANNABEL: Don't.

JOSH: Because you took a bottle of pills, didn't you, Bell?

RAE: What?

JOSH: You think cause we're guys that we just sit around looking for a hole to stick it in? He's my friend. We talk. But you didn't expect that did you? He told me he pulled you out of the bathtub and took you to the hospital.

ANNABEL: That was a long time ago.

JOSH: So that gives you a reason to forget? He saved your ass and kept your secret. (/)

ANNABEL: (/) I didn't know.

JOSH: (/) And you decided that you were too big to talk to people from home anymore. He was good enough to be your friend when they were pumping your stomach, wasn't he? You owe him your life and all he asked for was a long distance call. (/)

ANNABEL: (/) OK. OK. OK! I fucked up! What do you want me to say? I'm selfish? I'm a horrible person?

JOSH: I just want you to cut the bullshit!

ANNABEL: I...I... I was there, doing my thing. I wasn't even thinking about...and I...don't expect that there's this message waiting for me in my apartment when I get home from a hell day. I just don't think that...I like to know what's coming and I didn't know that his voice would...be there when I got home. I...was...the subway and the street car and my bag full of papers to mark and laundry and his voice...I was terrified. I thought no way. And I erased it.

RAE: Terrified? Of what?

ANNABEL: Hearing his voice... It was so...unexpected and it was like everything...came back to me. How I used to hate my life. God, there were months on end that I just had nothing to look forward to. I was always comparing myself to others. What they had, that they were loved, the way they looked and I was never as good. Everything was sad, birthdays, holidays...everywhere I looked I saw sadness. Old people made me sad because they seemed so hopeless. Just waiting to die alone and babies, they've just come into this miserable world to suffer alone. I wanted to stop the going around and around in my mind. Thoughts that wouldn't stop. And...and... He found me sinking in a bathtub.

RAE: Oh Annabel... That's so horrible.

ANNABEL: He held my hand when they made me drink this liquid charcoal stuff to soak up all the pills in my stomach. And it was his voice telling the nurse to stop asking me questions. He drove me home and helped me pack my stuff and got me out of Regina cause he knew it was killing me to stay. And not the city, but the place. All the disappointment of who I'd become was dripping from that place. So Clarky got me out. Even though he wanted me to stay. And so when I heard his message from so far away in my apartment... *(Pause.)* I panicked. I thought it was kind of weird that he was calling, yes, and then I thought, I have nothing to say to him cause...fuck!... I'm not the same person I was, so it's going to be all uncomfortable and what have you been up to and me making myself sound all busy and important and him sounding exactly the same and that makes me sick ok? It just does. Because he...his voice is this place to me and the way he sounded...is...me. The old me and...I didn't call him back.

RAE: People don't kill themselves because you erase their messages.

Silence.

I wish you would have called me.

ANNABEL: Why?

RAE: Why? Because I could have helped.

Pause.

JOSH: I'm going to go check on Clarky.

JOSH exits. Pause.

RAE: You don't think I could have helped?

ANNABEL: You weren't around, Rae. You were busy with your other life.

RAE: Just because I had other friends you make it sound like... Look, I had other friends because I needed more than one.

ANNABEL: Why?

RAE: Because...because all we ever did was smoke pot and talk about all the terrible atrocities in the world. It was a little heavy for me.

ANNABEL: You wanted to talk about that stuff as much as I did.

RAE: Fine. But then I also wanted to have fun and go dancing.

ANNABEL: And go shopping and get into bars when you were 16 and snort free coke.

RAE: There was a little of that, yes. You make me sound so shallow. It wasn't that.

ANNABEL: What was it then?

RAE: It was just different than what you wanted to do. It was work being your friend.

ANNABEL: Because I had opinions?

RAE: OK, when we were friends we analyzed lyrics and read Jeanette Winterson and Aldous Huxley. I loved being with you with but I had no idea where I was going or what I was doing.

ANNABEL: And your other friends did?

RAE: When I started hanging around with Cory and Leanne and those other guys…

ANNABEL: It was easy.

RAE: Yes it was. They all knew what they were going to do and as long as I was with them so did I.

ANNABEL: And that's what you did.

RAE: Then I met Robert.

ANNABEL: And then you married him…

RAE: We got the house, then I had Kiera and then Rebbah. It was so simple and clear cut.

ANNABEL: But?

RAE: But when Robert… When I found all the dirty e-mails…well it isn't what I planned and all of a sudden I was off track and the stupid fucking dance of anger…they haven't come out with the dance of a husband dipping his thing in a 25-year-old junior architect. *(Pause.)* Last week I was picking up Rebbah from C.K.C.—Creative Kids Camp—and I started to cry in front of her teenaged instructor. It was dreadful and they just stood there until Rebbah came over to me and put her little hand on my head and she said, "It's OK, Mommy, I'll be your friend." And I realized I...I didn't have a friend and I used to. So, *(Pause.)* I knew you'd be here. That's the truth. I miss you. You said before about not wanting to rescue me. I don't want you to. I just want to know that you're here or out there somewhere and...and that you still think of me...the way I think of you.

ANNABEL: I think about you but it's usually annoying thoughts about how happy you are.

RAE: I'm not.

ANNABEL: I know that now. *(Pause.)* I try to think of us at 15, when we still had good taste in music and we would smoke cigarettes and write stories together by finishing each other's sentences.

RAE: I still have that Split Enz album with all the weird shapes right on the record. *True Colours.*

ANNABEL: Oh yeah. It's got "Shark Attack" on it right?

RAE: Yeah that's the one.

ANNABEL: Teddy used to play that song in his car. No it was "I Got You."

RAE: *(She hums a little of the song.)* Did he ever talk about me?

ANNABEL: Uh...

RAE: People always felt more comfortable talking to you.

ANNABEL: I'm a commoner. Well, he used to go on and on about how pretty you were and how he couldn't

	believe you were going out with him out of all the guys.
RAE:	Really?
ANNABEL:	And he said he wished you were less into Bowie and more into Pink Floyd.
RAE:	We used to argue about that.
ANNABEL:	I'm sure. He loved to argue.
RAE:	Voted most likely to succeed in business. Everyone thought he'd be a lawyer.
ANNABEL:	But he wanted to be a teacher.
RAE:	He never felt good enough. Even back in high school. He didn't see himself the way we saw him.
ANNABEL:	No.
RAE:	Did you love him?
ANNABEL:	Sure. Yes.
RAE:	Me too.

      Silence.

Do you think Houston Pizza delivers to hospitals?

ANNABEL:	Probably.

      Pause.

RAE:	(*Humming the song. Pause.*) Do you remember how that song went.?
ANNABEL:	(*Thinking.*) No.

      Beat.

RAE:	(*Kind of tired, drunk singing.*) "I got you and that's what I want. I don't know why I don't know…" Shit.

ANNABE: Sorry.

RAE: I hate it when I just have to know something. Do you ever get that?

ANNABEL: I'm doing my thesis aren't I?

RAE: *(Giggles. Making fun of herself.)* Well, it's probably cheaper than couples counselling. *(Beat.)* Which is obviously working like a charm.

             ANNABEL laughs.

RAE: *(Kind of singing.)* "I got you, and that's what I want. Sometimes I get…I got you…"

ANNABEL: Shouldn't it be "I *have* you"?

RAE: They're from New Zealand.

ANNABEL: Ah.

RAE: Oh, I know, uh, "You can see my size, you can spell…you can spell a word like lightning. Da da da da."

ANNABEL: Not sure that's it.

RAE: It's not lightning.

ANNABEL: …people don't write songs about spelling. Even in the 80s. Even people from New Zealand. Spelling doesn't really get radio play.

RAE: "I got you. That's all I want. I got a doubt. That's all I know."

ANNABEL: *(Laughs.)* It's getting worse.

RAE: "You can see my size you can spell… I don't know why sometimes I get frightened."

ANNABEL: That sounds close. I'm having a flashback of you with your hair short on one side and long on the other.

RAE: Hey, you cut it. "I don't know why sometimes I get frightened. You can spell my name, you can spell..."

ANNABEL: "I get frightened... You can..."

                JOSH enters.

RAE: "You can see my size, you can spell..."

JOSH: *(Tentatively.)* How's it going?

ANNABEL: Josh will know.

JOSH: Know what?

RAE: We've been trying to figure out this song. "I don't know why sometimes I get frightened..." Something about spelling... You know it.

JOSH: Uh... "Sometimes we shout, shout shout shout!—but that's no problem. I don't know why sometimes I get frightened. You can see my eyes, you can tell that I'm not lyin'."

RAE: Yes! Oh my God.

ANNABEL: That's it.

RAE: Thank you so much. That was killing me.

ANNABEL: I can't believe you remember that song. I'm starting to think that pot *helps* your memory.

JOSH: ...*(Chuckle.)* Hey, I keep saying legalize...

                All laugh.

                (Chuckle.) ...you know, yesterday I blew into town and had eggs at the Low Quality Tea Room with Clarky.

RAE: How was he?

JOSH: Stoked to play hockey with me and my brother. We were going to meet in a couple of hours at the rink but he never showed up, so I went to his place after shooting the puck around for a bit and there were cop cars there... And an ambulance was peeling out. The cops were standing next to the garage smoking butts and writing stuff down. When I asked what they were doing they just said they had to air it out. The garage. That was all they said so I piled over to the nearest hospital to see him. They gave him the night so I crawled home, smoked a bowl before bed last night and then I don't know. It was pretty rank.

ANNABEL: What happened?

JOSH: Well, last night I had this dream. I wake up, you know in the dream and I go start the car like I always do and I blast into town and then...it's so quiet. Like everything's normal you know but not right. Something's missing. I go to Buns Master and there's some old guys in there smoking and then I go by Southland Mall to the Hellmart and there's all old ladies and their grandkids shopping and... It's all cool. You know. A boring kind of dream. And then I realize what the problem is. I look around and I'm the only one who's my age. You know? Anywhere. The city is totally cleaned out of people from 19 to I don't know...40. They're all gone. So I fall back asleep and I try to have the same dream but to fix it you know? And when I blow into town this time, it's totally empty. Everything is still there but the people are all gone and when I drive by Spears Funeral home on College...you know which one I mean?

RAE: Yes...

JOSH: Well on a sign you know a marquee out front...it says like about a hundred or so names. It's like I'm reading the fucking yearbook. They're all dead and I know that I'm the only one left to say anything over the coffins. And I think…you fuckers. You left me here. This place is a shit-fest without any people. You know? At least if everyone died I'd get my pick of the cars. Heavy eh? Did you ever study anything like that in university?

ANNABEL: Dream analysis isn't my field.

RAE: I could help you if there was some dancing in your dream.

JOSH: No chance of that. Yeah. *(Chuckles.)* Stupid dream eh? Next time I'll just wake and bake instead. Forget the whole thing. *(Beat.)* I know you guys think that I'm the tower of loser cause I stayed in Regina. I worked in a bar in Greece for four months.

RAE: You did?

JOSH: Yeah, I did. But I missed Reggie. Why would I leave anyway? Guys all over the world are dying to get what I got. House, car, girls… Family. Friends. *(Pause.)* Who else in your life do you have this with?

RAE: God…no one in Vancouver but that's because I don't really go out without the kids. And pot and Irish whiskey aren't really conducive to kids. Not kids from Vancouver anyway. *(Pause.)* It's more of a smack town I think.

> *Small laugh. RAE hands JOSH the empty bottle of whiskey.*

Sorry.

> *They look at her.*

JOSH: Nice work.

> *Pause.*

RAE: It's kind of calming. I mean it's chaos, my life.

Robert won't be there when I get home and I'll have to make up some creative thing to tell the girls. *(Making fun of herself.)* Where's Daddy? Where's Dad? He's gone to live at a motel with someone just a bit older than you girls! He left Mommy cause she was fat and that made Daddy feel like he was aging. Oh Daddy, you've still got it. We love you this much. *(Sigh.)* I'd have to change the hand movements (Beat.) ...but still...I feel calm right now. I'm sure it won't last.

JOSH: So stay a couple days extra and recharge your batteries here.

RAE: My mother would love that and I could really use a drink. Another drink. *(Beat.)* We're getting old aren't we?

JOSH: I'm kinda stoked cause we get to see how everything turns out.

            Pause.

ANNABEL: It's funny. When I come home I walk down the back alleys, alleys that would never exist in Toronto and I think maybe all my friends will still be playing back there like we used to. Planning great things on our bikes and avoiding our parents. Our secret streets just for us to ride on. And I somehow believe that if I turn the right corner or look in the right backyard then...I'll find them all back there. Just as I left them.

            Pause.

            Why do so many people from Regina stay friends?

RAE: I think your answer lies in your question.

            Pause.

JOSH: I spoke to the doctor. They said it's going to be a while before we can see him.

ANNABEL: I should really get back to my thesis.

RAE: I should go check on the girls.

JOSH: I better get more papers.

Pause. No one is going anywhere. Lights go out slowly. Music comes up.

The End.